6 Full-Length MCAS Grade 5 Math Practice Tests

Extra Test Prep to Help Ace the MCAS Grade 5 Math Test

By

Michael Smith & Reza Nazari

6 Full-Length MCAS Grade 5 Math Practice Tests

Published in the United State of America By

The Math Notion

Web: WWW.MathNotion.Com

Email: info@Mathnotion.com

About the Author

Michael Smith has been a math instructor for over a decade now. He holds a master's degree in Management. Since 2006, Michael has devoted his time to both teaching and developing exceptional math learning materials. As a Math instructor and test prep expert, Michael has worked with thousands of students. He has used the feedback of his students to develop a unique study program that can be used by students to drastically improve their math score fast and effectively.

- **SAT Math Practice Book**
- **ACT Math Practice Book**
- **GRE Math Practice Book**
- **Common Core Math Practice Book**
- **many Math Education Workbooks, Exercise Books and Study Guides**

As an experienced Math teacher, Mr. Smith employs a variety of formats to help students achieve their goals: He tutors online and in person, he teaches students in large groups, and he provides training materials and textbooks through his website and through Amazon.

You can contact Michael via email at:

info@Mathnotion.com

Prepare for the MCAS Grade 5 Math test with a perfect practice book!

The surest way to practice your MCAS Math test-taking skills is with simulated exams. This comprehensive practice book with 6 full length and realistic MCAS Math practice tests help you measure your exam readiness, find your weak areas, and succeed on the MCAS Math test. The detailed answers and explanations for each MCAS Math question help you master every aspect of the MCAS Math.

6 Full-length MCAS Grade 5 Math Practice Tests is a prestigious resource to help you succeed on the MCAS Math test. This perfect practice book features:

- Content 100% aligned with the MCAS test
- Six full-length MCAS Math practice tests similar to the actual test in length, format, question types, and degree of difficulty
- Detailed answers and explanations for the MCAS Math practice questions
- Written by MCAS Math top instructors and experts

After completing this hands-on exercise book, you will gain confidence, strong foundation, and adequate practice to succeed on the MCAS Math test.

WWW.MathNotion.COM

… So Much More Online!

✓ FREE Math Lessons

✓ More Math Learning Books!

✓ Mathematics Worksheets

✓ Online Math Tutors

For a PDF Version of This Book

Please Visit WWW.MathNotion.com

Contents

MCAS Math Practice Tests

Time to Test

Time to refine your skill with a practice examination

Take a REAL MCAS Mathematics test to simulate the test day experience. After you've finished, score your test using the answer key.

Before You Start

- You'll need a pencil and scratch papers to take the test.
- For this practice test, don't time yourself. Spend time as much as you need.
- It's okay to guess. You won't lose any points if you're wrong.
- After you've finished the test, review the answer key to see where you went wrong.

Calculators are not permitted for Grade 5 MCAS Tests

Good Luck!

Massachusetts Comprehensive Assessment System Grade 5

Mathematics Reference Sheet

CONVERSIONS

1 cup = 8 fluid ounces   1 mile = 5280 feet   1 pound = 16 ounces

1 pint = 2 cups   1 mile = 1760 yards   1 ton = 2000 pounds

1 quart = 2 pints

1 gallon = 4 quarts

AREA (A) FORMULAS

square . . . . $A = s \times s$

(s = length of a side)

rectangle . . . . . $A = b \times h$

(b = length of base; h = height)

OR

$A = l \times w$

(l = length; w = width)

VOLUME (V) FORMULAS

right rectangular prism . . . . $V = l \times w \times h$

(l = length; w = width; h = height)

OR

$V = B \times h$

(B = area of base; h = height)

Massachusetts Comprehensive Assessment System

MCAS Practice Test 1

Mathematics

GRADE 5

Administered *Month Year*

Session 1

❖ **Calculators are NOT permitted for this practice test.**

❖ **Time for Session 1: 85 Minutes**

1) A baker uses 3 eggs to bake a cake. How many cakes will he be able to bake with 210 eggs?

A. 65

B. 70

C. 56

D. 45

2) The area of a rectangle is D square feet and its length is 7 feet. Which equation represents W, the width of the rectangle in feet?

A. $W = \dfrac{D}{7}$

B. $W = \dfrac{7}{D}$

C. $W = 7D$

D. $W = 7 + D$

3) Which list shows the fractions in order from least to greatest?

$$\frac{3}{4}, \frac{6}{7}, \frac{2}{10}, \frac{1}{2}, \frac{6}{14}$$

A. $\dfrac{3}{4}, \dfrac{6}{7}, \dfrac{2}{10}, \dfrac{1}{2}, \dfrac{6}{14}$

B. $\dfrac{6}{14}, \dfrac{1}{2}, \dfrac{3}{4}, \dfrac{6}{7}, \dfrac{2}{10}$

C. $\dfrac{2}{10}, \dfrac{3}{4}, \dfrac{6}{7}, \dfrac{1}{2}, \dfrac{6}{14}$

D. $\dfrac{2}{10}, \dfrac{6}{14}, \dfrac{1}{2}, \dfrac{3}{4}, \dfrac{6}{7}$

4) If A = 30, then which of the following equations are correct?

     A. A + 30 = 60

     B. A ÷ 30 = 60

     C. 30 × A = 60

     D. A – 30 = 60

5) Which statement about 5 multiplied by $\frac{4}{3}$ is true?

     A. The product is between 3 and 4

     B. The product is between 6 and 7

     C. The product is more than $\frac{11}{3}$

     D. The product is between $\frac{14}{3}$ and 5

6) The area of a circle is 36π. What is the circumference of the circle?

Write your answer in the box below.

7) What is the volume of this box?

     A. 50 cm^3

     B. 62 cm^3

     C. 45 cm^3

     D. 120 cm^3

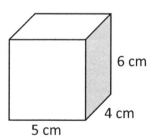

6 cm

4 cm

5 cm

8) A shirt costing $150 is discounted 10%. Which of the following expressions can be used to find the selling price of the shirt?

   A. $(150)(0.70)$

   B. $(150) - 150(0.30)$

   C. $(150)(0.15) - (150)(0.15)$

   D. $(150)(0.9)$

9) In a bag, there are 40 cards. Of these cards, 8 cards are white. What fraction of the cards are white?

   A. $\frac{1}{5}$

   B. $\frac{4}{10}$

   C. $\frac{32}{40}$

   D. $\frac{2}{20}$

10) The perimeter of the trapezoid below is 50. What is its area?

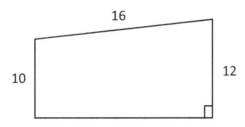

Write your answer in the box below.

Session 2

❖ **Calculators are NOT permitted for this practice test.**

❖ **Time for Session 2: 85 Minutes**

11) A rope weighs 500 grams per meter of length. What is the weight in kilograms of 12.2 meters of this rope? (1 kilograms = 1000 grams)

A. 0.061

B. 0.61

C. 6.1

D. 6,100

12) 10 yards 3 feet and 4 inches equals to how many inches?

Write your answer in the box below.

[ ]

13) Which expression has a value of – 7?

A. $7 - (-3) + (-17)$

B. $1 + (-3) \times (-2)$

C. $-6 \times (-6) + (-2) \times (-12)$

D. $(-2) \times (-7) + 4$

14) Of the 3,600 videos available for rent at a certain video store, 900 are comedies. What percent of the videos are comedies?

A. 18 ½ %

B. 20%

C. 22%

D. 25%

MCAS Math Practice Tests – Grade 5

15) The length of a rectangle is $\frac{5}{6}$ of inches and the width of the rectangle is $\frac{2}{15}$ of inches. What is the area of that rectangle?

A. $\frac{1}{2}$

B. $\frac{1}{9}$

C. $\frac{20}{24}$

D. $\frac{5}{24}$

16) William keeps track of the length of each fish that he catches. Following are the lengths in inches of the fish that he caught one day: 15, 16, 9, 14, 9, 10, 18

What is the median fish length that William caught that day?

A. 18 Inches

B. 9 Inches

C. 10 Inches

D. 14 Inches

17) Solve. $\frac{1}{2} + \frac{4}{7} - \frac{1}{14} =$

A. $\frac{9}{10}$

B. $\frac{2}{10}$

C. 1

D. 14

18) If one acre of forest contains 150 pine trees, how many pine trees are contained in 30 acres?

A. 450

B. 1,500

C. 4,500

D. 45,000

19) How many $\frac{1}{4}$ cup servings are in a package of cheese that contains $5\frac{1}{2}$ cups altogether?

A. $5\frac{1}{8}$

B. $\frac{11}{8}$

C. 11

D. 22

20) The area of the base of the following cylinder is 60 square inches and its height is 10 inches. What is the volume of the cylinder?

Write your answer in the box below.

"This is the end of Practice Test 1"

Massachusetts Comprehensive Assessment System

MCAS Practice Test 2

Mathematics

GRADE 5

Administered *Month Year*

Session 1

❖ **Calculators are NOT permitted for this practice test.**

❖ **Time for Session 1: 85 Minutes**

1) Jack added 16 to the product of 14 and 22. What is this sum?

   A. 86

   B. 336

   C. 324

   D. 7,602

2) Joe makes $4.75 per hour at his work. If he works 6 hours, how much money will he earn?

   A. $33.00

   B. $32.75

   C. $36.50

   D. $28.5

3) Which of the following is an obtuse angle?

   A. 89°

   B. 66°

   C. 150°

   D. 240°

4) What is the value of $5 - 3\frac{2}{9}$?

   A. $\frac{23}{9}$

   B. $1\frac{7}{9}$

   C. $-\frac{1}{9}$

   D. $\frac{42}{9}$

5) The bride and groom invited 230 guests for their wedding. 190 guests arrived. What percent of the guest list was not present?

A. 70%

B. 40%

C. 43.32%

D. 17.40%

6) In a party, 8 soft drinks are required for every 12 guests. If there are 156 guests, how many soft drinks are required?

A. 18

B. 36

C. 104

D. 171

7) You are asked to chart the temperature during an 8–hour period to give the average. These are your results:

7 am: 3 degrees   11 am: 31 degrees

8 am: 6 degrees   12 pm: 34 degrees

9 am: 23 degrees   1 pm: 34 degrees

10 am: 29 degrees   2 pm: 32 degrees

What is the average temperature?

A. 24

B. 28

C. 36

D. 46

8) While at work, Emma checks her email once every 90 minutes. In 12 hours, how many times does she check her email?

Write your answer in the box below.

9) A florist has 585 flowers. How many full bouquets of 13 flowers can he make?

Write your answer in the box below.

10) What is 6,123.48245 rounded to the nearest tenth?

   A. 6,123.482

   B. 6,123.5

   C. 6,123

   D. 6,123.48

Session 2

❖ **Calculators are NOT permitted for this practice test.**

❖ **Time for Session 2: 85 Minutes**

11) What is the volume of the following rectangle prism?

A. $15\ ft^3$

B. $20\ ft^3$

C. $24\ ft^3$

D. $210\ ft^3$

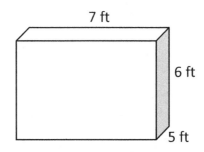

12) A circle has a diameter of 4 inches. What is its approximate circumference? (π = 3.14)

A. 6.23 inches

B. 12.56 inches

C. 32.65 inches

D. 36.12 inches

13) How long is the line segment shown on the number line below?

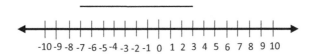

A. 10

B. 9

C. 8

D. 7

14) Peter traveled 160 miles in 4 hours and Jason traveled 240 miles in 8 hours.

What is the ratio of the average speed of Peter to average speed of Jason?

A. 4: 3

B. 2: 3

C. 5: 7

D. 5: 6

15) If $x = -2$, which equation is true?

A. $x(2x - 4) = 50$

B. $8(4 - x) = 48$

C. $2(4x + 6) = 10$

D. $6x - 2 = -23$

16) What are the coordinates of the intersection of x-$axis$ and the y-$axis$ on a coordinate plane?

A. (5, 5)

B. (1, 1)

C. (0, 0)

D. (0, 1)

17) In a triangle ABC the measure of angle ACB is 35° and the measure of angle CAB is 65°. What is the measure of angle ABC?

Write your answer in the box below.

18) Which list shows the fractions listed in order from least to greatest?

$$\frac{1}{3}, \frac{1}{10}, \frac{1}{6}, \frac{1}{8}$$

A. $\frac{1}{8}, \frac{1}{3}, \frac{1}{10}, \frac{1}{6}$

B. $\frac{1}{6}, \frac{1}{10}, \frac{1}{3}, \frac{1}{8}$

C. $\frac{1}{3}, \frac{1}{6}, \frac{1}{8}, \frac{1}{10}$

D. $\frac{1}{10}, \frac{1}{8}, \frac{1}{6}, \frac{1}{3}$

19) If a rectangular swimming pool has a perimeter of 124 feet and it is 24 feet wide, what is its area?

Write your answer in the box below.

20) Aria was hired to teach three identical 5th grade math courses, which entailed being present in the classroom 24 hours altogether. At $20 per class hour, how much did Aria earn for teaching one course?

A. $50

B. $160

C. $300

D. $1,400

"This is the end of Practice Test 2"

Massachusetts Comprehensive Assessment System

MCAS Practice Test 3

Mathematics

GRADE 5

Administered *Month Year*

Session 1

❖ **Calculators are NOT permitted for this practice test.**

❖ **Time for Session 1: 85 Minutes**

21) A baker uses 4 eggs to bake a cake. How many cakes will he be able to bake with 240 eggs?

A. 15

B. 60

C. 240

D. 960

22) The area of a rectangle is D square feet and its length is 5 feet. Which equation represents W, the width of the rectangle in feet?

A. $W = \dfrac{D}{5}$

B. $W = \dfrac{5}{D}$

C. $W = 5D$

D. $W = 5 + D$

23) Which list shows the fractions in order from least to greatest?

$$\frac{2}{5}, \frac{7}{8}, \frac{3}{10}, \frac{1}{4}, \frac{8}{18}$$

A. $\dfrac{2}{5}, \dfrac{7}{8}, \dfrac{3}{10}, \dfrac{1}{4}, \dfrac{8}{18}$

B. $\dfrac{8}{18}, \dfrac{1}{4}, \dfrac{2}{5}, \dfrac{7}{8}, \dfrac{3}{10}$

C. $\dfrac{3}{10}, \dfrac{2}{5}, \dfrac{7}{8}, \dfrac{1}{4}, \dfrac{8}{18}$

D. $\dfrac{1}{4}, \dfrac{3}{10}, \dfrac{2}{5}, \dfrac{8}{18}, \dfrac{7}{8}$

24) If A = 40, then which of the following equations are correct?

    A. A + 40 = 80

    B. A ÷ 40 = 80

    C. 40 × A = 80

    D. A – 40 = 80

25) Which statement about 6 multiplied by $\frac{5}{4}$ is true?

    A. The product is between 6 and 7

    B. The product is between 7 and 8

    C. The product is more than $\frac{25}{3}$

    D. The product is between $\frac{17}{3}$ and 6

26) The area of a circle is 64π. What is the circumference of the circle?

Write your answer in the box below.

27) What is the volume of this box?

    A. 42 cm^3

    B. 21 cm^3

    C. 12 cm^3

    D. 84 cm^3

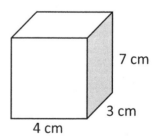

28) A shirt costing $170 is discounted 20%. Which of the following expressions can be used to find the selling price of the shirt?

A. (170) (0.90)

B. (170) – 170 (0.40)

C. (170) (0.10) – (170) (0.10)

D. (170) (0.8)

29) In a bag, there are 50 cards. Of these cards, 6 cards are white. What fraction of the cards are white?

A. $\frac{3}{25}$

B. $\frac{4}{25}$

C. $\frac{44}{50}$

D. $\frac{2}{50}$

30) The perimeter of the trapezoid below is 60. What is its area?

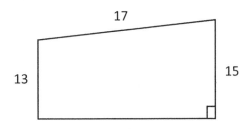

Write your answer in the box below.

Session 2

❖ **Calculators are NOT permitted for this practice test.**

❖ **Time for Session 2: 85 Minutes**

31) A rope weighs 600 grams per meter of length. What is the weight in kilograms of 15.5 meters of this rope? (1 kilograms = 1000 grams)

A. 0.093

B. 0.93

C. 9.3

D. 9,300

32) 12 yards 5 feet and 8 inches equals to how many inches?

Write your answer in the box below.

```
┌─────────────────────────┐
│                         │
└─────────────────────────┘
```

33) Which expression has a value of – 8?

A. $5 - (-6) + (-19)$

B. $-3 + (-4) \times (-3)$

C. $-7 \times (-5) + (-3) \times (-11)$

D. $(-3) \times (-5) + 1$

34) Of the 4,200 videos available for rent at a certain video store, 840 are comedies.

What percent of the videos are comedies?

A. $18\frac{2}{3}\%$

B. 25%

C. 22%

D. 20%

35) The length of a rectangle is $\frac{4}{5}$ of inches and the width of the rectangle is $\frac{7}{8}$ of inches. What is the area of that rectangle?

A. $\frac{1}{2}$

B. $\frac{7}{10}$

C. $\frac{11}{40}$

D. $\frac{5}{10}$

36) William keeps track of the length of each fish that he catches. Following are the lengths in inches of the fish that he caught one day: 11, 16, 10, 15, 8, 10, 20

What is the median fish length that William caught that day?

A. 8 Inches

B. 20 Inches

C. 10 Inches

D. 11 Inches

37) Solve. $\frac{2}{3} + \frac{5}{7} - \frac{8}{21} =$

A. $\frac{15}{31}$

B. $\frac{15}{63}$

C. 1

D. 0

38) If one acre of forest contains 120 pine trees, how many pine trees are contained in 45 acres?

    A. 540

    B. 4,500

    C. 5,400

    D. 54,000

39) How many $\frac{1}{6}$ cup servings are in a package of cheese that contains $6\frac{1}{3}$ cups altogether?

    A. $6\frac{1}{6}$

    B. $\frac{11}{6}$

    C. 11

    D. 38

40) The area of the base of the following cylinder is 40 square inches and its height is 12 inches. What is the volume of the cylinder?

Write your answer in the box below.

"This is the end of Practice Test 3"

Massachusetts Comprehensive Assessment System

MCAS Practice Test 4

Mathematics

GRADE 5

Administered *Month Year*

Session 1

❖ **Calculators are NOT permitted for this practice test.**

❖ **Time for Session 1: 85 Minutes**

1) Jack added 20 to the product of 11 and 25. What is this sum?

   A. 56

   B. 275

   C. 295

   D. 5,500

2) Joe makes $5.25 per hour at his work. If he works 8 hours, how much money will he earn?

   A. $33

   B. $52

   C. $36

   D. $42

3) Which of the following is an obtuse angle?

   A. 89°

   B. 45°

   C. 170°

   D. 210°

4) What is the value of $8 - 4\frac{3}{7}$?

   A. $\frac{23}{7}$

   B. $3\frac{4}{7}$

   C. $-\frac{4}{7}$

   D. $\frac{24}{7}$

5) The bride and groom invited 250 guests for their wedding. 203 guests arrived. What percent of the guest list was not present?

A. 70%

B. 30%

C. 81.20%

D. 18.80%

6) In a party, 12 soft drinks are required for every 20 guests. If there are 200 guests, how many soft drinks are required?

A. 20

B. 36

C. 120

D. 166

7) You are asked to chart the temperature during an 8–hour period to give the average. These are your results:

7 am: 4 degrees   11 am: 25 degrees

8 am: 5 degrees   12 pm: 32 degrees

9 am: 16 degrees   1 pm: 36 degrees

10 am: 20 degrees   2 pm: 38 degrees

What is the average temperature?

A. 22

B. 21.5

C. 24

D. 17.25

8) While at work, Emma checks her email once every 70 minutes. In 14 hours, how many times does she check her email?

Write your answer in the box below.

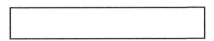

9) A florist has 750 flowers. How many full bouquets of 15 flowers can he make?

Write your answer in the box below.

10) What is 7,234.57326 rounded to the nearest tenth?

A. 7,234.573

B. 7,234.6

C. 7,234

D. 7,234.57

Session 2

❖ **Calculators are NOT permitted for this practice test.**

❖ **Time for Session 2: 85 Minutes**

11) What is the volume of the following rectangle prism?

A. 32 ft^3

B. 20 ft^3

C. 40 ft^3

D. 160 ft^3

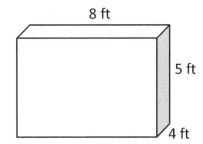

12) A circle has a diameter of 6 inches. What is its approximate circumference? (π = 3.14)

A. 9.42 inches

B. 18.84 inches

C. 32.65 inches

D. 37.68 inches

13) How long is the line segment shown on the number line below?

A. 7

B. 10

C. 3

D. 5

14) Peter traveled 180 miles in 6 hours and Jason traveled 360 miles in 9 hours.

What is the ratio of the average speed of Peter to average speed of Jason?

A. 3: 4

B. 2: 3

C. 5: 8

D. 9: 4

15) If $x = -4$, which equation is true?

A. $x(5x - 10) = 60$

B. $7(6 - x) = 70$

C. $3(2x + 16) = 10$

D. $4x - 12 = -25$

16) What are the coordinates of the intersection of $x-axis$ and the $y-axis$ on a coordinate plane?

A. $(-1, -1)$

B. $(1, 1)$

C. $(0, 0)$

D. $(0, 1)$

17) In a triangle ABC the measure of angle ACB is 45° and the measure of angle CAB is 60°. What is the measure of angle ABC?

Write your answer in the box below.

18) Which list shows the fractions listed in order from least to greatest?

$$\frac{1}{4}, \frac{1}{11}, \frac{1}{7}, \frac{1}{9}$$

A. $\frac{1}{9}, \frac{1}{4}, \frac{1}{11}, \frac{1}{7}$

B. $\frac{1}{7}, \frac{1}{11}, \frac{1}{4}, \frac{1}{9}$

C. $\frac{1}{4}, \frac{1}{7}, \frac{1}{9}, \frac{1}{11}$

D. $\frac{1}{11}, \frac{1}{9}, \frac{1}{7}, \frac{1}{4}$

19) If a rectangular swimming pool has a perimeter of 160 feet and it is 35 feet wide, what is its area?

Write your answer in the box below.

20) Aria was hired to teach five identical 5th grade math courses, which entailed being present in the classroom 25 hours altogether. At $25 per class hour, how much did Aria earn for teaching one course?

A. $150

B. $125

C. $625

D. $3,125

"This is the end of Practice Test 4"

Massachusetts Comprehensive Assessment System

MCAS Practice Test 5

Mathematics

GRADE 5

Administered *Month Year*

Session 1

❖ **Calculators are NOT permitted for this practice test.**

❖ **Time for Session 1: 85 Minutes**

1) A baker uses 5 eggs to bake a cake. How many cakes will he be able to bake with 250 eggs?

    A. 20

    B. 50

    C. 250

    D. 950

2) The area of a rectangle is D square feet and its length is 8 feet. Which equation represents W, the width of the rectangle in feet?

    A. $W = \dfrac{D}{8}$

    B. $W = \dfrac{8}{D}$

    C. $W = 8D$

    D. $W = 8 + D$

3) Which list shows the fractions in order from least to greatest?

$$\frac{7}{10}, \frac{8}{9}, \frac{3}{5}, \frac{2}{16}, \frac{1}{2}$$

    A. $\dfrac{3}{5}, \dfrac{8}{9}, \dfrac{1}{2}, \dfrac{2}{16}, \dfrac{7}{10}$

    B. $\dfrac{7}{10}, \dfrac{2}{16}, \dfrac{3}{5}, \dfrac{8}{9}, \dfrac{1}{2}$

    C. $\dfrac{1}{2}, \dfrac{3}{5}, \dfrac{8}{9}, \dfrac{2}{16}, \dfrac{7}{10}$

    D. $\dfrac{2}{16}, \dfrac{1}{2}, \dfrac{3}{5}, \dfrac{7}{10}, \dfrac{8}{9}$

4) If A = 30, then which of the following equations are correct?

    A. A + 30 = 60

    B. A ÷ 30 = 60

    C. 30 × A = 60

    D. A − 30 = 60

5) Which statement about 3 multiplied by $\frac{7}{2}$ is true?

    A. The product is between 8 and 9

    B. The product is between 10 and 11

    C. The product is more than $\frac{35}{2}$

    D. The product is between $\frac{15}{2}$ and 8

6) The area of a circle is 81π. What is the circumference of the circle?

Write your answer in the box below.

7) What is the volume of this box?

    A. 16 cm^3

    B. 16 cm^3

    C. 40 cm^3

    D. 80 cm^3

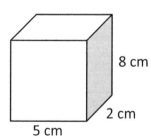

8 cm

2 cm

5 cm

8) A shirt costing $140 is discounted 15%. Which of the following expressions can be used to find the selling price of the shirt?

    A. (140) (0.80)

    B. (140) – 140 (0.85)

    C. (140) (0.15) – (140) (0.15)

    D. (140) (0.85)

9) In a bag, there are 60 cards. Of these cards, 8 cards are white. What fraction of the cards are white?

    A. $\dfrac{2}{15}$

    B. $\dfrac{7}{15}$

    C. $\dfrac{16}{60}$

    D. $\dfrac{2}{60}$

10) The perimeter of the trapezoid below is 40. What is its area?

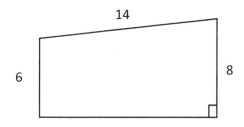

Write your answer in the box below.

Session 2

❖ **Calculators are NOT permitted for this practice test.**

❖ **Time for Session 2: 85 Minutes**

11) A rope weighs 300 grams per meter of length. What is the weight in kilograms of 12.6 meters of this rope? (1 kilograms = 1000 grams)

A. 0.0378

B. 0.378

C. 3.78

D. 3,780

12) 7 yards 6 feet and 10 inches equals to how many inches?

Write your answer in the box below.

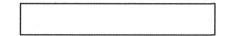

13) Which expression has a value of – 11?

A. $7 - (-3) + (-21)$

B. $-4 + (-6) \times (-5$

C. $-5 \times (-8) + (-2) \times (-6)$

D. $(-4) \times (-7) + 2$

14) Of the 3,400 videos available for rent at a certain video store, 680 are comedies.

What percent of the videos are comedies?

A. $20\frac{2}{5}\%$

B. 24%

C. 12%

D. 20%

15) The length of a rectangle is $\frac{3}{8}$ of inches and the width of the rectangle is $\frac{5}{9}$ of

inches. What is the area of that rectangle?

A. $\frac{1}{3}$

B. $\frac{5}{24}$

C. $\frac{11}{24}$

D. $\frac{15}{24}$

16) William keeps track of the length of each fish that he catches. Following are

the lengths in inches of the fish that he caught one day: 6, 11, 5, 10, 3, 5, 15

What is the median fish length that William caught that day?

A. 3 Inches

B. 15 Inches

C. 5 Inches

D. 6 Inches

17) Solve. $\frac{1}{4} + \frac{5}{6} - \frac{2}{24} =$

A. $\frac{15}{24}$

B. $\frac{11}{24}$

C. 1

D. 2

18) If one acre of forest contains 110 pine trees, how many pine trees are contained in 26 acres?

A. 286

B. 8,260

C. 2,860

D. 28,600

19) How many $\frac{1}{8}$ cup servings are in a package of cheese that contains $5\frac{1}{4}$ cups altogether?

A. $5\frac{1}{4}$

B. $\frac{14}{5}$

C. 12

D. 42

20) The area of the base of the following cylinder is 45 square inches and its height is 8 inches. What is the volume of the cylinder?

Write your answer in the box below.

"This is the end of Practice Test 3"

Massachusetts Comprehensive Assessment System

MCAS Practice Test 6

Mathematics

GRADE 5

Administered *Month Year*

Session 1

❖ **Calculators are NOT permitted for this practice test.**

❖ **Time for Session 1: 85 Minutes**

1) Jack added 18 to the product of 12 and 15. What is this sum?

    A. 89

    B. 981

    C. 198

    D. 2,198

2) Joe makes $4.75 per hour at his work. If he works 5 hours, how much money will he earn?

    A. $30.25

    B. $35.25

    C. $33.50

    D. $23.75

3) Which of the following is an obtuse angle?

    A. 69°

    B. 35°

    C. 150°

    D. 200°

4) What is the value of $6 - 3\frac{2}{5}$?

    A. $\frac{25}{9}$

    B. $2\frac{3}{5}$

    C. $-\frac{1}{5}$

    D. $\frac{13}{5}$

5) The bride and groom invited 265 guests for their wedding. 222 guests arrived. What percent of the guest list was not present?

A. 90%

B. 20%

C. 26.24%

D. 16.23%

6) In a party, 16 soft drinks are required for every 30 guests. If there are 240 guests, how many soft drinks are required?

A. 18

B. 48

C. 128

D. 158

7) You are asked to chart the temperature during an 8–hour period to give the average. These are your results:

7 am: 5 degrees	11 am: 25 degrees
8 am: 6 degrees	12 pm: 34 degrees
9 am: 14 degrees	1 pm: 35 degrees
10 am: 21 degrees	2 pm: 36 degrees

What is the average temperature?

A. 22

B. 22.5

C. 23

D. 19.25

8) While at work, Emma checks her email once every 30 minutes. In 11 hours, how many times does she check her email?

Write your answer in the box below.

9) A florist has 720 flowers. How many full bouquets of 18 flowers can he make?

Write your answer in the box below.

10) What is 3,458.56817 rounded to the nearest tenth?

A. 3,458.568

B. 3,458.6

C. 3,458

D. 3,458.56

Session 2

❖ **Calculators are NOT permitted for this practice test.**

❖ **Time for Session 2: 85 Minutes**

11) What is the volume of the following rectangle prism?

A. $63\ ft^3$

B. $33\ ft^3$

C. $66\ ft^3$

D. $198\ ft^3$

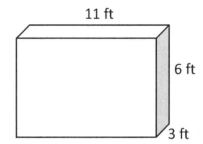

12) A circle has a diameter of 4 inches. What is its approximate circumference? ($\pi = 3.14$)

A. 6.28 inches

B. 12.56 inches

C. 24.56 inches

D. 33.28 inches

13) How long is the line segment shown on the number line below?

B. 8

B. 12

C. 6

D. 4

14) Peter traveled 240 miles in 8 hours and Jason traveled 550 miles in 11 hours.

What is the ratio of the average speed of Peter to average speed of Jason?

   A. 3: 5

   B. 5: 3

   C. 5: 9

   D. 9: 5

15) If $x = -7$, which equation is true?

   A. $x(2x + 8) = 50$

   B. $2(9 - x) = 32$

   C. $5(4x + 18) = 17$

   D. $2x - 18 = -35$

16) What are the coordinates of the intersection of $x-axis$ and the $y-axis$ on a coordinate plane?

   A. $(-5, -5)$

   B. $(5, 5)$

   C. $(0, 0)$

   D. $(0, 5)$

17) In a triangle ABC the measure of angle ACB is $65°$ and the measure of angle CAB is $50°$. What is the measure of angle ABC?

Write your answer in the box below.

18) Which list shows the fractions listed in order from least to greatest?

$$\frac{1}{2}, \frac{1}{17}, \frac{1}{3}, \frac{1}{8}$$

A. $\frac{1}{8}, \frac{1}{2}, \frac{1}{17}, \frac{1}{3}$

B. $\frac{1}{3}, \frac{1}{17}, \frac{1}{2}, \frac{1}{9}$

C. $\frac{1}{2}, \frac{1}{8}, \frac{1}{3}, \frac{1}{17}$

D. $\frac{1}{17}, \frac{1}{8}, \frac{1}{3}, \frac{1}{2}$

19) If a rectangular swimming pool has a perimeter of 80 feet and it is 25 feet wide, what is its area?

Write your answer in the box below.

20) Aria was hired to teach seven identical 4th grade math courses, which entailed being present in the classroom 35 hours altogether. At $32 per class hour, how much did Aria earn for teaching one course?

A. $120

B. $160

C. $610

D. $1,116

"This is the end of Practice Test 6"

Answer Keys

MCAS Practice Tests

❋ Now, it's time to review your results to see where you went wrong and what areas you need to improve!

Practice Test - 1				Practice Test - 2			
1	B	11	C	1	C	11	D
2	A	12	400	2	D	12	B
3	D	13	A	3	C	13	A
4	A	14	D	4	B	14	A
5	B	15	B	5	D	15	B
6	12π	16	D	6	C	16	C
7	D	17	C	7	A	17	80°
8	D	18	C	8	8	18	D
9	A	19	D	9	45	19	912
10	132	20	600	10	B	20	B

Practice Test - 3

1	B	11	C
2	A	12	500
3	D	13	A
4	A	14	D
5	B	15	B
6	16π	16	D
7	D	17	C
8	D	18	C
9	A	19	D
10	210	20	480

Practice Test - 4

1	C	11	D
2	D	12	B
3	C	13	A
4	B	14	A
5	D	15	B
6	C	16	C
7	A	17	75°
8	12	18	D
9	50	19	1,575
10	B	20	B

Practice Test - 5

1	B	11	C
2	A	12	334
3	D	13	A
4	A	14	D
5	B	15	B
6	18π	16	D
7	D	17	C
8	D	18	C
9	A	19	D
10	84	20	360

Practice Test - 6

1	C	11	D
2	D	12	B
3	C	13	A
4	B	14	A
5	D	15	B
6	C	16	C
7	A	17	65°
8	22	18	D
9	40	19	375
10	B	20	B

Answers and Explanations

Practice Test 1

MCAS - Mathematics

Answers and Explanations

1) Answer: B.

3 eggs for 1 cake. Therefore, 210 eggs can be used for (210 ÷ 3) 70 cakes.

2) Answer: A.

Use area of rectangle formula.

$$area\ of\ a\ rectangle\ =\ width \times length \Rightarrow D = w \times l \Rightarrow w = \frac{D}{l} = \frac{D}{7}$$

3) Answer: D.

To list the fractions from least to greatest, you can convert the fractions to decimal.

$$\frac{3}{4} = 0.75; \frac{6}{7} = 0.86; \frac{2}{10} = 0.2; \frac{1}{2} = 0.5; \frac{6}{14} = 0.43$$

$$\frac{2}{10} = 0.2, \frac{6}{14} = 0.43, \frac{1}{2} = 0.5, \frac{3}{4} = 0.75, \frac{6}{7} = 0.86$$

Option D shows the fractions in order from least to greatest.

4) Answer: A.

Plug in 30 for A in the equations. Only option A works.

$$A + 30 = 60 \Rightarrow 30 + 30 = 60$$

5) Answer: B.

5 multiplied by $\frac{4}{3} = \frac{20}{3} = 6.66$, therefore, only choice B is correct.

6) Answer: 12π.

Use area and circumference of circle formula.

Area of a circle $= \pi r^2 \Rightarrow 36\pi = \pi r^2 \Rightarrow r = 6$

Circumference of a circle $= 2\pi r \Rightarrow C = 2 \times 6 \times \pi \Rightarrow C = 12\pi$

7) Answer: D.

Use volume of rectangle formula.

$$Volume\ of\ a\ rectangle\ =\ width \times length \times heigth$$

$$\Rightarrow V = 4 \times 5 \times 6 \Rightarrow V = 120$$

8) Answer: D.

To find the selling price, multiply the price by (100% – rate of discount).

Then: (150) (100% – 10%) = (150) (0.9) = 135

9) Answer: A.

There are 40 cards in the bag and 8 of them are white. Then, 8 out of 40 cards are white.

You can write this as: $\frac{8}{40}$. To simplify this fraction, divide both numerator and

denominator by 13. Then: $\frac{8}{40} = \frac{1}{5}$

10) Answer: 132.

First, find the missing side of the trapezoid. The perimeter of the trapezoid below is 50.

Therefore, the missing side of the trapezoid (its height) is:

$50 - 10 - 16 - 12 = 50 - 38 = 12$

Area of a trapezoid: A $= \frac{1}{2}$ h (b1 + b2)

$= \frac{1}{2}$ (12) (10 + 12) = 132

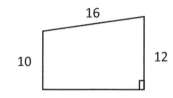

11) Answer: C.

1 meter of the rope = 500 grams

12.2 meter of the rope = 12.2 × 500 = 6,100grams = 6.1 kg

12) Answer: 400.

10 yards = 10 × 36 = 360 inches

3 feet = 3 × 12 = 36 inches

10 yards 3 feet and 4 inches = 360 inches + 36 inches + 4 inches = 400 inches

13) Answer: A.

Simplify each option provided using order of operations rules.

A.7 – (– 3) + (– 17) = 7 + 3 – 17 = –7

B.1 + (– 3) × (– 2) = 1 + 6 = 7

C.– 6 × (– 6) + (– 2) × (– 12) = 36 + 24 = 60

D.(– 2) × (– 7) + 4 = 14 + 4 = 18

Only option A is –7.

14) Answer: D.

Use percent formula: $\text{part} = \frac{\text{percent}}{100} \times \text{whole}$

$900 = \frac{\text{percent}}{100} \times 3600 \Rightarrow 900 = \text{percent} \times 36 \Rightarrow \text{percent} = 25$

15) Answer: B.

Use area of rectangle formula.

$Area = length \times width \Rightarrow A = \frac{5}{6} \times \frac{2}{15} \Rightarrow A = \frac{1}{9}$ inches

16) Answer: D.

Write the numbers in order: 9, 9, 10, 14, 15, 16, 18

Median is the number in the middle. Therefore, the median is 14.

17) Answer: C.

$\frac{1}{2} + \frac{4}{7} - \frac{1}{14} = \frac{(7 \times 1) + (2 \times 4) - (1 \times 1)}{14} = \frac{14}{14} = 1$

18) Answer: C.

1 acre: 150 pine trees

30 acres: $150 \times 30 = 4{,}500$ pine trees

19) Answer: D.

To solve this problem, divide $5\frac{1}{2}$ by $\frac{1}{4}$.

$5\frac{1}{2} \div \frac{1}{4} = \frac{11}{2} \div \frac{1}{4} = \frac{11}{2} \times \frac{4}{1} = 22$

20) Answer: 600.

Use volume of cylinder formula.

$Voluem = base \times heigth \Rightarrow V = 60 \times 10 \Rightarrow V = 600$

Practice Test 2

MCAS - Mathematics

Answers and Explanations

1) Answer: C.

$16 + (14 \times 22) = 16 + 308 = 324$

2) Answer: D.

1 hour: \$4.75; 6 hours: $6 \times \$4.75 = \$28.5$

3) Answer: C.

An obtuse angle is an angle of greater than 90° and less than 180°. From the options provided, only option C (150 degrees) is an obtuse angle.

4) Answer: B.

$5 - 3\frac{2}{9} = \frac{45}{9} - \frac{29}{9} = \frac{16}{9} = 1\frac{7}{9}$

5) Answer: D.

The number of guests that are not present are: $(230 - 190)$ 40 out of $230 = \frac{40}{230}$

Change the fraction to percent: $\frac{40}{230} \times 100\% = 17.4\%$

6) Answer: C.

Write a proportion and solve.

$\frac{8 \text{ soft drinks}}{12 \text{ guests}} = \frac{x}{156 \text{ guests}} \Rightarrow x = \frac{156 \times 8}{12} \Rightarrow x = 104$

7) Answer: A.

$\text{average (mean)} = \frac{\text{sum of terms}}{\text{number of terms}} \Rightarrow \text{average} = \frac{3+6+23+29+31+34+34+32}{8} \Rightarrow \text{average} = 24$

8) Answer: 8.

Every 90 minutes Emma checks her email.

In 12 hours (720 minutes), Emma checks her email $(720 \div 90)$ 8 times.

9) Answer: 45.

Divide the number flowers by 13: $585 \div 13 = 45$

10) Answer: B.

Rounding decimals is similar to rounding other numbers. If the hundredths and thousandths places of a decimal is forty-nine or less, they are dropped, and the tenths place does not change. For example, rounding 0.843 to the nearest tenth would give 0.8. Therefore, 6,123.48245 rounded to the nearest tenth is 6,123.5.

11) Answer: D.

Use volume of rectangle prism formula.

$$V = length \times width \times height \Rightarrow V = 7 \times 5 \times 6 \Rightarrow V = 210$$

12) Answer: B.

The diameter of the circle is 4 inches. Therefore, the radius of the circle is 2 inches.

Use circumference of circle formula: $C = 2\pi r \Rightarrow C = 2 \times 3.14 \times 2 \Rightarrow C = 12.56$

13) Answer: A.

The line segment is from 3 to -7. Therefore, the line is 9 units. $3 - (-7) = 3 + 7 = 10$

14) Answer: A.

Peter's speed $= \dfrac{160}{4} = 40$

Jason's speed $= \dfrac{240}{8} = 30$

$\dfrac{The\ average\ speed\ of\ peter}{The\ average\ speed\ of\ Jason} = \dfrac{40}{30}$ equals to: $\dfrac{4}{3}$ or $4:3$

15) Answer: B.

Plug in $x = -2$ in each equation.

A. $x(2x - 4) = 50 \rightarrow (-2)(2(-2) - 4) = (-2) \times (-4 - 4) = 16$

B. $8(4 - x) = 48 \rightarrow 8(4 - (-2)) = 8(6) = 48$

C. $2(4x + 6) = 10 \rightarrow 2(4(-2) + 6) = 2(-8 + 6) = -4$

D. $6x - 2 = -23 \rightarrow 6(-2) - 2 = -12 - 2 = -14$

Only option B.

16) Answer: C.

The horizontal axis in the coordinate plane is called the $x - axis$. The vertical axis is called the $y - axis$. The point at which the two axes intersect is called the origin. The origin is at 0 on the $x - axis$ and 0 on the $y - axis$.

17) Answer: 80°.

All angles in every triangle add up to $180°$. Let x be the angle ABC.

Then: $180 = 65 + 35 + x \Rightarrow x = 80°$

18) Answer: D.

In fractions, when denominators increase, the value of fractions decrease and as much as numerators increase, the value of fractions increase. Therefore, the least one of this list is: $\frac{1}{10}$ and the greatest one of this list is: $\frac{1}{3}$

19) Answer: 912.

Perimeter of rectangle formula:

$P = 2 \, (length + width) \Rightarrow 124 = 2 \, (l + 24) \Rightarrow l = 38$

Area of rectangle formula: $A = length \times width \Rightarrow A = 38 \times 24 \Rightarrow A = 912$

20) Answer: B.

Aria teaches 24 hours for three identical courses. Therefore, she teaches 8 hours for each course. Aria earns $20 per hour. Therefore, she earned $160 ($8 \times 20$) for each course.

Practice Test 3

MCAS - Mathematics

Answers and Explanations

1) Answer: B.

4 eggs for 1 cake. Therefore, 240 eggs can be used for $(240 \div 4)$ 60 cakes.

2) Answer: A.

Use area of rectangle formula.

$$area\ of\ a\ rectangle\ =\ width \times length \Rightarrow D = w \times l \Rightarrow w = \frac{D}{l} = \frac{D}{5}$$

3) Answer: D.

To list the fractions from least to greatest, you can convert the fractions to decimal.

$$\frac{2}{5} = 0.4; \frac{7}{8} = 0.875; \frac{3}{10} = 0.3; \frac{1}{4} = 0.25; \frac{8}{18} = 0.444$$

$$\frac{1}{4} = 0.25, \frac{3}{10} = 0.3, \frac{2}{5} = 0.4, \frac{8}{18} = 0.444, \frac{7}{8} = 0.875$$

Option D shows the fractions in order from least to greatest.

4) Answer: A.

Plug in 40 for A in the equations. Only option A works.

$$A + 40 = 80 \Rightarrow 40 + 40 = 80$$

5) Answer: B.

6 multiplied by $\frac{5}{4} = \frac{30}{4} = 7.5$, therefore, only choice B is correct.

6) Answer: 16π.

Use area and circumference of circle formula.

Area of a circle $= \pi r^2 \Rightarrow 64\pi = \pi r^2 \Rightarrow r = 8$

Circumference of a circle $= 2\pi r \Rightarrow C = 2 \times 8 \times \pi \Rightarrow C = 16\pi$

7) Answer: D.

Use volume of rectangle formula.

$$Volume\ of\ a\ rectangle\ =\ width \times length \times heigth \Rightarrow V = 3 \times 4 \times 7 \Rightarrow V = 84$$

8) Answer: D.

To find the selling price, multiply the price by (100% – rate of discount).

Then: (170) (100% – 20%) = (170) (0.8) = 136

9) Answer: A.

There are 50 cards in the bag and 6 of them are white. Then, 6 out of 50 cards are white.

You can write this as: $\frac{6}{50}$. To simplify this fraction, divide both numerator and

denominator by 2. Then: $\frac{6}{50} = \frac{3}{25}$

10) Answer: 210.

First, find the missing side of the trapezoid. The perimeter of the trapezoid below is 60.

Therefore, the missing side of the trapezoid (its height) is:

60 – 13 – 17 – 15 = 60 – 45 = 15

Area of a trapezoid: $A = \frac{1}{2}h\,(b1 + b2)$

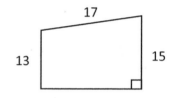

$= \frac{1}{2}(15)\,(13 + 15) = 210$

11) Answer: C.

1 meter of the rope = 600 grams

15.5 meter of the rope = 15.5 × 600 = 9,300grams = 9.3 kg

12) Answer: 500.

12 yards = 12 × 36 = 432 inches

5 feet = 5 × 12 = 60 inches

12 yards 5 feet and 8 inches = 432 inches + 60 inches + 8 inches = 500 inches

13) Answer: A.

Simplify each option provided using order of operations rules.

A. 5 – (– 6) + (– 19) = 5 + 6 – 19 = –8

B. –3 + (– 4) × (– 3) = –3 + 12 = 9

C. – 7 × (– 5) + (– 3) × (– 11) = 35 + 33 = 68

D. (– 3) × (– 5) + 1 = 15 + 1 = 16

Only option A is –8.

14) Answer: D.

Use percent formula: part $= \frac{\text{percent}}{100} \times$ whole

$840 = \frac{\text{percent}}{100} \times 4,200 \Rightarrow 840 = \text{percent} \times 42 \Rightarrow \text{percent} = 20$

15) Answer: B.

Use area of rectangle formula.

$Area = length \times width \Rightarrow A = \frac{4}{5} \times \frac{7}{8} \Rightarrow A = \frac{7}{10}$ *inches*

16) Answer: D.

Write the numbers in order: 8, 10, 10, 11, 15, 16, 20

Median is the number in the middle. Therefore, the median is 11.

17) Answer: C.

$\frac{2}{3} + \frac{5}{7} - \frac{8}{21} = \frac{(7 \times 2) + (3 \times 5) - (1 \times 8)}{21} = \frac{21}{21} = 1$

18) Answer: C.

1 acre: 120 pine trees

45 acres: $120 \times 45 = 5,400$ pine trees

19) Answer: D.

To solve this problem, divide $6\frac{1}{3}$ by $\frac{1}{6}$.

$6\frac{1}{3} \div \frac{1}{6} = \frac{19}{3} \div \frac{1}{6} = \frac{19}{3} \times \frac{6}{1} = 38$

20) Answer: 480.

Use volume of cylinder formula.

$Voluem = base \times heigth \Rightarrow V = 40 \times 12 \Rightarrow V = 480$

Practice Test 4

MCAS - Mathematics

Answers and Explanations

1) Answer: C.

$20 + (11 \times 25) = 20 + 275 = 295$

2) Answer: D.

1 hour: $5.25; 8 hours: $8 \times \$5.25 = \$42$

3) Answer: C.

An obtuse angle is an angle of greater than 90° and less than 180°. From the options provided, only option C (170 degrees) is an obtuse angle.

4) Answer: B.

$8 - 4\frac{3}{7} = \frac{56}{7} - \frac{31}{7} = \frac{25}{7} = 3\frac{4}{7}$

5) Answer: D.

The number of guests that are not present are: $(250 - 203)$ 47 out of $230 = \frac{47}{250}$

Change the fraction to percent: $\frac{47}{250} \times 100\% = 18.8\%$

6) Answer: C.

Write a proportion and solve.

$\frac{12 \text{ soft drinks}}{20 \text{ guests}} = \frac{x}{200 \text{ guests}} \Rightarrow x = \frac{200 \times 12}{20} \Rightarrow x = 120$

7) Answer: A.

$\text{average (mean)} = \frac{\text{sum of terms}}{\text{number of terms}} \Rightarrow \text{average} = \frac{4+5+16+20+25+32+36+38}{8} \Rightarrow \text{average} = 22$

8) Answer: 12.

Every 70 minutes Emma checks her email.

In 14 hours (840 minutes), Emma checks her email $(840 \div 70)$ 12 times.

9) Answer: 50.

Divide the number flowers by 15: $750 \div 15 = 50$

10) Answer: B.

Rounding decimals is similar to rounding other numbers. If the hundredths and thousandths places of a decimal is fifty-eight or less, they are dropped, and the tenths place does not change. For example, rounding 0.843 to the nearest tenth would give 0.8. Therefore, 7,234.57326 rounded to the nearest tenth is 7,234.6.

11) Answer: D.

Use volume of rectangle prism formula.

$$V = length \times width \times height \Rightarrow V = 8 \times 4 \times 5 \Rightarrow V = 160$$

12) Answer: B.

The diameter of the circle is 6 inches. Therefore, the radius of the circle is 3 inches.

Use circumference of circle formula: $C = 2\pi r \Rightarrow C = 2 \times 3.14 \times 3 \Rightarrow C = 18.84$

13) Answer: A.

The line segment is from 5 to -2. Therefore, the line is 7 units.

$$5 - (-2) = 5 + 2 = 7$$

14) Answer: A.

Peter's speed $= \frac{180}{6} = 30;$ 　　　　　　　　Jason's speed $= \frac{360}{9} = 40$

$\frac{The\ average\ speed\ of\ peter}{The\ average\ speed\ of\ Jason} = \frac{30}{40}$ equals to: $\frac{3}{4}$ or $3:4$

15) Answer: B.

Plug in $x = -4$ in each equation.

A. $x(5x - 10) = 60 \rightarrow (-4)(5(-4) - 10) = (-4) \times (-20 - 10) = 120$

B. $7(6 - x) = 70 \rightarrow 7(6 - (-4) = 7(10) = 70$

C. $3(2x + 16) = 10 \rightarrow 3(2(-4) + 16) = 3(-8 + 16) = 24$

D. $4x - 12 = -25 \rightarrow 4(-4) - 12 = -16 - 12 = -28$

Only option B.

16) Answer: C.

The horizontal axis in the coordinate plane is called the $x-axis$. The vertical axis is called the $y-axis$. The point at which the two axes intersect is called the origin. The origin is at 0 on the $x-axis$ and 0 on the $y-axis$.

17) Answer: 75°.

All angles in every triangle add up to $180°$. Let x be the angle ABC.

Then: $180 = 60 + 45 + x \Rightarrow x = 75°$

18) Answer: D.

In fractions, when denominators increase, the value of fractions decrease and as much as numerators increase, the value of fractions increase. Therefore, the least one of this list is: $\frac{1}{11}$ and the greatest one of this list is: $\frac{1}{4}$

19) Answer: 1,575.

Perimeter of rectangle formula:

$P = 2 \, (length + width) \Rightarrow 160 = 2 \, (l + 35) \Rightarrow l = 45$

Area of rectangle formula: $A = length \times width \Rightarrow A = 45 \times 35 \Rightarrow A = 1,575$

20) Answer: B.

Aria teaches 25 hours for five identical courses. Therefore, she teaches 5 hours for each course. Aria earns \$25 per hour. Therefore, she earned \$125 (5×25) for each course.

Practice Test 5

MCAS - Mathematics

Answers and Explanations

1) Answer: B.

5 eggs for 1 cake. Therefore, 250 eggs can be used for $(250 \div 5)$ 50 cakes.

2) Answer: A.

Use area of rectangle formula.

$$area \ of \ a \ rectangle \ = \ width \times length \Rightarrow D = w \times l \Rightarrow w = \frac{D}{l} = \frac{D}{8}$$

3) Answer: D.

To list the fractions from least to greatest, you can convert the fractions to decimal.

$$\frac{3}{5} = 0.6; \frac{8}{9} = 0.889; \frac{7}{10} = 0.7; \frac{1}{2} = 0.5; \frac{2}{16} = 0.125$$

$$\frac{2}{16} = 0.125, \frac{1}{2} = 0.5, \frac{3}{5} = 0.6, \frac{7}{10} = 0.7, \frac{8}{9} = 0.889$$

Option D shows the fractions in order from least to greatest.

4) Answer: A.

Plug in 30 for A in the equations. Only option A works.

$$A + 30 = 60 \Rightarrow 30 + 30 = 60$$

5) Answer: B.

3 multiplied by $\frac{7}{2} = \frac{21}{2} = 10.5$, therefore, only choice B is correct.

6) Answer: 18π.

Use area and circumference of circle formula.

Area of a circle $= \pi r^2 \Rightarrow 81\pi \ = \ \pi r^2 \Rightarrow r = 9$

Circumference of a circle $= 2\pi r \ \Rightarrow C \ = \ 2 \times 9 \times \pi \ \Rightarrow C \ = 18\pi$

7) Answer: D.

Use volume of rectangle formula.

$$Volume \ of \ a \ rectangle \ = \ width \times length \times heigh \Rightarrow V = 5 \times 2 \times 8 \Rightarrow V = 80$$

8) Answer: D.

To find the selling price, multiply the price by (100% – rate of discount).

Then: (140) (100% – 15%) = (140) (0.85) = 119

9) Answer: A.

There are 60 cards in the bag and 8 of them are white. Then, 8 out of 60 cards are white.

You can write this as: $\frac{8}{60}$. To simplify this fraction, divide both numerator and

denominator by 4. Then: $\frac{8}{60} = \frac{2}{15}$

10) Answer: 84.

First, find the missing side of the trapezoid. The perimeter of the trapezoid below is 40.

Therefore, the missing side of the trapezoid (its height) is:

40 – 6 – 8 – 14 = 40 – 28 = 12

Area of a trapezoid: $A = \frac{1}{2} h \, (b1 + b2)$

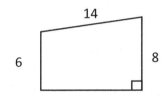

$= \frac{1}{2} (12) (6 + 8) = 84$

11) Answer: C.

1 meter of the rope = 300 grams

12.6 meter of the rope = 12.6 × 300 = 3,780 grams = 3.78 kg

12) Answer: 334.

7 yards = 7 × 36 = 252 inches

6 feet = 6 × 12 = 72 inches

7 yards 6 feet and 10 inches = 252 inches + 72 inches + 10 inches = 334 inches

13) Answer: A.

Simplify each option provided using order of operations rules.

A. 7 – (– 3) + (– 21) = 7 + 3 – 21 = –11

B. –4 + (– 6) × (– 5) = –4 + 30 = 26

C. – 5 × (– 8) + (– 2) × (– 6) = 40 + 12 = 52

D. (– 4) × (– 7) + 2 = 28 + 2 = 30

Only option A is –11.

14) Answer: D.

Use percent formula: $\text{part} = \dfrac{\text{percent}}{100} \times \text{whole}$

$680 = \dfrac{\text{percent}}{100} \times 3{,}400 \Rightarrow 680 = \text{percent} \times 34 \Rightarrow \text{percent} = 20$

15) Answer: B.

Use area of rectangle formula.

$Area = length \times width \Rightarrow A = \dfrac{3}{8} \times \dfrac{5}{9} \Rightarrow A = \dfrac{5}{24} \ inches$

16) Answer: D.

Write the numbers in order: 3, 5, 5, 6, 10, 11, 15

Median is the number in the middle. Therefore, the median is 6.

17) Answer: C.

$\dfrac{1}{4} + \dfrac{5}{6} - \dfrac{2}{24} = \dfrac{(6\times1)+(4\times5)-(1\times2)}{24} = \dfrac{24}{24} = 1$

18) Answer: C.

1 acre: 110 pine trees

26 acres: $110 \times 26 = 2{,}860$ pine trees

19) Answer: D.

To solve this problem, divide $5\dfrac{1}{4}$ by $\dfrac{1}{8}$.

$5\dfrac{1}{4} \div \dfrac{1}{8} = \dfrac{21}{4} \div \dfrac{1}{8} = \dfrac{42}{8} \times \dfrac{8}{1} = 42$

20) Answer: 360.

Use volume of cylinder formula.

$Voluem = base \times heigth \Rightarrow V = 45 \times 8 \Rightarrow V = 360$

Practice Test 6

MCAS - Mathematics

Answers and Explanations

1) Answer: C.

$18 + (12 \times 15) = 18 + 180 = 198$

2) Answer: D.

1 hour: \$4.75; 5 hours: $5 \times \$4.75 = \$23.75$

3) Answer: C.

An obtuse angle is an angle of greater than 90° and less than 180°. From the options provided, only option C (150 degrees) is an obtuse angle.

4) Answer: B.

$6 - 3\frac{2}{5} = \frac{30}{5} - \frac{17}{5} = \frac{13}{5} = 2\frac{3}{5}$

5) Answer: D.

The number of guests that are not present are: $(265 - 222)$ 43 out of $265 = \frac{43}{265}$

Change the fraction to percent: $\frac{43}{265} \times 100\% = 16.23\%$

6) Answer: C.

Write a proportion and solve.

$\frac{16 \text{ soft drinks}}{30 \text{ guests}} = \frac{x}{240 \text{ guests}} \Rightarrow x = \frac{240 \times 16}{30} \Rightarrow x = 128$

7) Answer: A.

$\text{average (mean)} = \frac{\text{sum of terms}}{\text{number of terms}} \Rightarrow \text{average} = \frac{5+6+14+21+25+34+35+36}{8} \Rightarrow \text{average} = 22$

8) Answer: 22.

Every 30 minutes Emma checks her email.

In 11 hours (660 minutes), Emma checks her email $(660 \div 30)$ 22 times.

9) Answer: 40.

Divide the number flowers by 18: $720 \div 18 = 40$

10) Answer: B.

Rounding decimals is similar to rounding other numbers. If the hundredths and thousandths places of a decimal is fifty-six or less, they are dropped, and the tenths place does not change. For example, rounding 0.843 to the nearest tenth would give 0.8. Therefore, 3,458.56817 rounded to the nearest tenth is 3,458.6.

11) Answer: D.

Use volume of rectangle prism formula.

$$V = length \times width \times height \Rightarrow V = 3 \times 6 \times 11 \Rightarrow V = 198$$

12) Answer: B.

The diameter of the circle is 4 inches. Therefore, the radius of the circle is 2 inches.

Use circumference of circle formula: $C = 2\pi r \Rightarrow C = 2 \times 3.14 \times 2 \Rightarrow C = 12.56$

13) Answer: A.

The line segment is from 4 to −4. Therefore, the line is 8 units.

$$4 - (-4) = 4 + 4 = 8$$

14) Answer: A.

Peter's speed $= \dfrac{240}{8} = 30;$ Jason's speed $= \dfrac{550}{11} = 50$

$\dfrac{The\ average\ speed\ of\ peter}{The\ average\ speed\ of\ Jason} = \dfrac{30}{50}$ equals to: $\dfrac{3}{5}$ or $3:5$

15) Answer: B.

Plug in $x = -7$ in each equation.

A. $x(2x + 8) = 50 \rightarrow (-7)(2(-7) + 8) = (-7) \times (-14 + 8) = 42$

B. $2(9 - x) = 32 \rightarrow 2(9 - (-7)) = 2(16) = 32$

C. $5(4x + 18) = 17 \rightarrow 5(4(-7) + 18) = 5(-28 + 18) = -50$

D. $2x - 18 = -35 \rightarrow 2(-7) - 18 = -14 - 18 = -32$

Only option B.

16) Answer: C.

The horizontal axis in the coordinate plane is called the $x - axis$. The vertical axis is called the $y - axis$. The point at which the two axes intersect is called the origin. The origin is at 0 on the $x - axis$ and 0 on the $y - axis$.

17) Answer: 65°.

All angles in every triangle add up to 180°. Let x be the angle ABC.

Then: $180 = 65 + 50 + x \Rightarrow x = 65°$

18) Answer: D.

In fractions, when denominators increase, the value of fractions decrease and as much as numerators increase, the value of fractions increase. Therefore, the least one of this list is: $\frac{1}{17}$ and the greatest one of this list is: $\frac{1}{2}$

19) Answer: 375.

Perimeter of rectangle formula:

$P = 2\,(length + width) \Rightarrow 80 = 2\,(l + 25) \Rightarrow l = 15$

Area of rectangle formula: $A = length \times width \Rightarrow A = 15 \times 25 \Rightarrow A = 375$

20) Answer: B.

Aria teaches 35 hours for seven identical courses. Therefore, she teaches 5 hours for each course. Aria earns $32 per hour. Therefore, she earned $160 ($5 \times 32$) for each course.

"End"

Made in United States
North Haven, CT
03 June 2022

19804006R00057